THE OWNER OF THE SEA

RICHARD PRICE has published over a dozen books of poetry since his debut in 1993, including *Lucky Day* (2005), which was a *Guardian* Book of the Year and shortlisted for the Whitbread Poetry Prize. Since then, every Carcanet collection he has published has been shortlisted for a major prize. In 2012 his poem 'Hedge Sparrows' was chosen to represent Team GB in the Olympics project 'The Written World'. A year later, *Small World*, won the Creative Scotland Award in his home country. It was followed by another *Guardian* Book of the Year, *Moon for Sale* (2017).

His poems have been widely anthologised and he has been translated into French, Finnish, German, Hungarian and Portuguese. He is a short story writer and novelist, and the editor of the little magazine *Painted, spoken*. He is the lyricist for the musical project The Loss Adjustors.

He is Head of Contemporary British Collections at the British Library, in London, which includes the Sound Archive, Publications, and Contemporary Archives and Manuscripts.

The Owner of the Sea

THREE INUIT STORIES

retold by

RICHARD PRICE

with an afterword by

NANCY CAMPBELL

CARCANET CLASSICS

First published in Great Britain in 2021 by
Carcanet
Alliance House, 30 Cross Street
Manchester M2 7AQ
www.carcanet.co.uk

A CIP catalogue record for this book is
available from the British Library.

ISBN 978 1 80017 117 6

Printed in Great Britain by SRP Ltd, Exeter, Devon

The publisher acknowledges financial
assistance from Arts Council England.

CONTENTS

2. After the Storm

3. The Spiders and the Beads

4. Smoke, or is it Steam?

5. Driftwood, Needle and Thread

6. If You Can't Be Good Be Careful

7. Grizzly

8. The Lake Spirit

9. The Fox-Wife

10. The Goose

INTRODUCTION

I first encountered the Inuit spiritual world when the artist Ronald King invited me to work on a book he was making about 'the owner of the sea', Sedna. The story of Sedna is of a woman defying her father and her society, of a wild creature taking advantage of Sedna's rebelliousness, and then of the severe punishment for her transgression. It is a beautiful and at the same time shocking creation story.

I immersed myself in accounts of Sedna and wrote the small number of poems that tell *Sedna and the Fulmar*. I didn't stop there, though; I began to write about her more fully, ending up with the sequence collected here. After a brief pause I began to read about other legends and tales and the result is this book, with Sedna and her father at the beginning and the hunter Kiviuq and his goose-wife at the close.

As I was to learn, Inuit narratives are not 'just stories': they are a way of seeing the world and the life within it. So much so that when I use words here like 'story' and 'narrative', 'myth' and 'legend', I use them with implicit tongs – like the tongs that try to deprive Kiviuq of his boots at a particularly awkward moment – knowing that these words are placeholders for better concepts I can't yet articulate or even fully understand. Even 'spiritual' doesn't sound right, because it wrongly suggests a division between a supernatural world and the natural one.

There are many and contradictory ways of reading these stories. That is one of their great gifts. This is particularly in regard to how men and women work, live and love together, especially in a society living at the extreme margins of survival. Such a society has evolved a division of labour in which men are expected, roughly speaking, to do a set of certain tasks and women, roughly speaking, another – while allowing and needing flexibility and overlap.

Clearly, and malignly, key decisions are reserved for men. The tales pull no punches in describing how fraught with the jeopardy of violent misogyny such a society can, at its worst, be. Yet they also prod and jab at the problem of individualism within a society which only has so much room for 'free will'. In any case, these are ancient stories and– bearing in mind the fuzzing of mythic and realistic modes we should be sensitive to in folk tales – the social norms they seem to imply are as long gone in Inuit cultures as any other (if they are long gone in other cultures…)

Perhaps it is actually best 'not to read' these tales when reading them: I can only encourage readers first to enjoy them, absorb them, take them in, rather than 'read' in the moral or literary sense, as a person might engage with any novel or film or song, taking in the story and the manner of its delivery– as you would horror, adventure, fantasy, tragedy, magic – in a spirit of receptivity which will judge only in that direct, fast-moving way any audience has in the moment. Let snagging analysis and judgement come later, if they must.

To that end I've tried to make these poems deliver something analogous to what I understand as the enigma and the energy of the originals, while also inevitably being different and other. There is no sense in which this book is a translation. Instead, this is a book of poems which take inspiration from prose texts published in English based on many Inuit-language versions of tales which were first rendered live hundreds and hundreds of years ago, as oral, told, stories. They are still rendered that way – in fact, more than rendered, that is what they *are*.

I have been especially inspired by the tales gathered from some forty elders in the first decade of the twenty-first century in the Kiviuq project, which Kira Van Deusen's team embarked on, and which she so illuminatingly documents and reflects upon in *Kiviuq: An Inuit Hero and His Siberian Cousins*. These are collected in the beautifully realised website *Kiviuq's*

Journey, www.unipka.ca. The anthropological writings by Boas and Rasmussen at least a century earlier are another source.

Taken together these stories, garnered from elders across large territories, can differ from each other in incidental detail and, just sometimes, on larger parts of a story. This has set a challenge for a poet attempting a straight line in the poetic sequence, so much so that sometimes I have resisted the straight line altogether, allowing the discontinuities to offer a breathing pause in the general flow.

Through Ronald King I was introduced to Frédéric Laugrand and Jarich Oosten's *The Sea Woman: Sedna in Inuit Shamanism and Art in the Eastern Arctic*, which has become another vital guide in my understanding of Inuit cultures. There is no single Sedna or Kiviuq story – they are stories which are as alive as some still believe Sedna and Kiviuq may be alive – and to be alive means to change, to be contradictory, to be individual, to be social, even to be mercurial. Storytelling of the kind witnessed in such accounts, and which is fundamental to the transmission of the stories down the generations, is an extremely sophisticated art. Its enduring power is testified to by the detailed survival of these tales over what is likely to be thousands of years.

Clearly the poetry inscribed in this published book is at several major removes from the original stories which inspired it. The poetry is no substitute for the stories, in the way that a religious painting would be no substitute for the sacred story it tries to depict (I think of north European paintings of the Renaissance period trying to stretch back well over a thousand years to imagine scenes from the New Testament, itself a written text trying to reach back to the spoken words of Christ, who, an Aramaic speaker living close to the southern Mediterranean, would not have spoken as a first language the Greek which the New Testament 'witnesses' him in. Yet who would gainsay the sincerity of the painter, or their ability to reach back to some part at least of the core of the Christian story?)

What the reader of this book can be sure of is that key events, where there is a commonly agreed order, are told in that order, and that no key events have been invented 'for the sake of dramatic effect'.

Sometimes I have chosen variants which may be less common in the tales but do exist. In the story of the Lake Spirit, in the present version, Kiviuq kills at one point by fire rather than by knife. The relationship between fire and life was interesting to me and I wanted to keep that less popular version. I have also suggested what I see as an understated bisexuality in Kiviuq – his wading out to the lake usually reports a swift death for the lake spirit but one earlier transcription might imply he has sex with it first. Similarly, his travelling song has variations in which the 'torsos' which are a challenge for him are described in different ways: specifically female; sexless; or simply 'buttocks'. This was enough for me to make just a little bit more of that part of the story and make both women and men who desire Kiviuq an 'obstacle' for him. I have made all the animals in the underworld female except for the siksik, whose sex traditionally Kiviuq has difficulty in distinguishing. Again, this seems interesting to me in terms of sexuality and I have made something of that.

I have chosen a style of poetry which is both very loose – syllabically, in conventions of lines per stanza, and so on – and yet tight, allowing context and a certain dead-pan modernism, a serial minimalism, to accentuate the weight of each of the situations in which each of the central characters finds themself. Shifts of perspective – where one character's voice is followed by another, or, in *Sedna*, people in the village speak as a brief chorus – are intended to give further interest to the whole, offering a dramatic and almost 'straight to camera' effect that is intended to help sustain the piece while avoiding one single voice or tone. Sometimes, as with the shifting gender of the pronouns in *The Old Woman*, I have engineered a grammatical change to signal one happening in the story itself; moves between tenses and between first person and third person are made where I have had particular and different intensities of story in mind. All that said, in general the brevity of each poem invites the reader to quickly skip to the next short text rather than get snagged in over-ornate versifying. These poems are meant to remember the narrative propulsion which inspired them in the first place.

In that respect I can't help but think of Kiviuq's travelling song, towards the end of his tale, in which he encounters a boiling cauldron with chunks of meat in it. This is an image we are given to believe is also an image of the sea and its fragments of floating ice. To complete his song-journey he has to step from one chunk to another as quickly as he can. My own poetry has often used this technique in the past – I have written in narrative sequences almost from the very first stirrings of my poetry vocation and have continued to do so throughout my poetic life – but the verse novels of Bernadine Evaristo (*The Emperor's Babe*) and Dorothy Porter (*The Monkey's Mask*) and the sequence *nora's place* by Tom Leonard have been particularly in my mind as I have been writing this book.

What is a departure in a structural way is that I have given much more attention to the voices of the women in the stories, writing dialogues and monologues for them which, as elsewhere in this book, have taken advantage of techniques from theatre and screen. Very occasionally a modern-day narrator's voice intervenes. I actually don't think this is against tradition to do so – storytellers modernise, contextualise, are sensitive to and ask questions of their audience, and they explain as well. Even so, I try not to be prim or prissy or over-didactic in so doing. Once only, the narrator appears where there is a critical divergence of the story among sources, taking advantage of that interpretative problem as a 'choice' for the audience to make (as it happens, the point in question is also focussed on a deeply shocking act). Where there are Inuit words I make it very clear in the context what these words are, sometimes 'doubling' the Inuit word with an English near-equivalent (as Robert Burns often does with Scots and English in his work) so that I don't have to footnote what is essentially a poetry drama.

I have occasionally allowed myself some fun with the stories – for example playing with the modern-day language of relationship-counselling in Kiviuq's first encounter with a woman – but this has been the exception. Some aspects of the story are naturally funny in any case, funny peculiar and funny ha ha, and I believe Inuit audiences are not po-faced (this is different from being fundamentally irreverent, which this set of sequences is not).

In the epic of Kiviuq there are strange shifts in time between the episodes, perhaps a result of their being separable as stories and so each having a hidden history of their own re-composition in re-telling. It is rare for either *Sedna* or *Kiviuq* to be performed as a single sequence. This may have led to apparent continuity errors. Does Kiviuq have more than one mother, for example? She seems to die fairly early on, only to reappear much later. When exactly was sea ice created? And so on.

Sometimes these do not need to be resolved, since the dream logic of ancient tales allows a lot of disjunction; the flashback device also has its uses. Once or twice, though, I've chosen a particular interpretation to make a coherence and even to suggest a rich spiritual and psychological life. In the case of the two mothers, I suggest the second is actually the dead presence of the first. As the tale of the goose-wife shows, she still manages to be a vocal and, in this case, sadly destructive part of the family, as if Kiviuq has not learnt to let her influence go. I also follow Kira Van Deusen and certain elders in strongly suggesting that the fox-wife is a reincarnation of one of the women Kiviuq kills, though I still leave this as a suggestion, not a categorical interpretation.

The most serious gap, to my mind, follows Kiviuq's reunion with the fox-wife. Some say they renewed their relationship, some say that the fox-wife slipped away again, and who could blame her? I felt the end of the underground sequence seems so final that I did not want to make any kind of coda for it, either a happy ever after or a downbeat recording of final parting. Instead I scripted a poem to open the next section, which tries to make a bridge between the fox-wife story and that of the goose. It is a simple reflection on the near-eternal youthfulness of Kiviuq and what that might mean for his ability to make connections to those who love him; and what that might mean for the mere mortals involved.

In this book, I've started with Sedna, a creation myth whose core is a female spirit or god. Then I've used the short narrative, *The Old Woman Who Changed Herself Into A Man* as a transition to the man-boy stories of the Kiviuq cycle. There are many other Inuit tales of course, but this introductory selection has, I hope, a certain narrative arc.

Earlier I said that there are many ways of reading these tales. I'd like to emphasise, though, two unambiguous truths which are central to them: that the life of creatures deserves our respect, and that human behaviour towards the creatures affects not only their well-being but our own.

Sadly, these truths have not been observed by Western society for hundreds of years and probably much longer. Ignorance of or contempt for the ecosystems of which we are certainly only a part has only accelerated in the current century, with mass extinctions and climate crisis the result. In recent decades the West has been joined in its consumption mania by the emerging superpowers of the East and the internally colonising giant of Brazil. The latter's elite prefers a short-term meat economy to the long-term survival of the planet. We really are all connected, and it is an injustice of planetary proportions that no people are more threatened by the insanely consuming behaviour of these self-indulgent territories than the distant Inuit.

The Arctic heathland burns, the ice disappears, the seas rise and the oceans have fewer and fewer creatures swimming in them: Sedna has already started to withhold her bounty. Kiviuq has not been seen for many a year and may already have turned to stone.

Select Bibliography

Franz Boas, *The Eskimo Of Baffin Land And Hudson Bay: From Notes Collected By George Comer, James S. Mutch, E.J. Peck, Volume 15, Part 1*, Wentworth Press, 2019.[reprinted from *Bulletin of the American Museum of Natural History*, 1907].

Frédéric Laugrand and Jarich Oosten, *The Sea Woman: Sedna in Inuit Shamanism and Art in the Eastern Arctic*, University of Alaska Press, 2010.

Knud Rasmussen, *Report of the Fifth Thule Expedition, 1921–1929, Vol 8: The Netsilik Eskimo: Social Life and Spiritual Culture*, Gyldendalske Boghandel, Nordisk Forlag. 1931.

Kira Van Deusen, *Kiviuq: An Inuit Hero and His Siberian Cousins*, McGill-Queen's University Press, 2009.

Kira Van Deusen (selector and editor), *Kiviuq's Journey*, www.unipka.ca. [2008].This site presents the Kiviuq's story in the words of forty Inuit elders, as part of a project by filmmaker John Houston and storyteller Kira Van Deusen. The elders were Elisapee Karlik, Bernadette Patterk, Naalungiaq Makkigaq, Mariano Aupilardjuk, Henry Isluanik, Peter

Suwaksiork, Phillip Kijusiutnerk, Samson Quinangnaq, Simon Tookoome, Leo Nimialik, Joe Issaluk, Theresa Kimaliardjuk, Eli Kimaliardjuk, Henry Evaluardjuk, Madeleine Ivalu, Rachel Ujarusuk, Sippora Inuksuk, Jacob Peterloosie, Cornelius Nutarak, Annie Peterloosie, Joanisee Macpa, Gideon Qitsualik, Mary Ittunga, Bernadette Uttaq, Frank Analok, Moses Koihok, Margaret Nakashuk, Madeleine Makkigaq, Ollie Ittinuar, Felix Kopak, Peter Katorka, Celestine Erkidjuk, Herve Paniaq, Naujarlak Tassugat, Judas Aqilgiaq, Jimmie Qiqut, Ruby Eleeheetook, Niviuvak Marqniq, and Matthew Nakashook.

Acknowledgements

My poems are in debt to the elders, authors and storytellers cited in the Select Bibliography as well as to more general reading. Some poems collected were first published in the artist's book *Sedna & The Fulmar* by Ronald King, who I am especially grateful to for introducing me to these worlds. Some of the poems here have been included in the anthology *Prototype: 1* edited by Jess Chandler, in *Wet Grain* edited by Patrick Romero and Christian Lemay, and in Michael Schmidt's *PN Review*. My thank you, too, to Michael, John McAuliffe, Andrew Latimer, Jazz Linklater and all at Carcanet, to Bill Broady, David Kinloch, Peter McCarey, and April Yee, who read versions of the text, and to Nancy Campbell for her *Afterword* and encouragement in this project.

THE OWNER OF THE SEA

THE OWNER OF THE SEA

Who remembers the names of the Owner of the Sea?

She is the Owner of the Sea,
The Woman Who Would Not Marry.
The One Who Did Not Want a Husband,
The Owner of the Sea.

She is the Woman Who Was Always Having Sex,
The Terrifying One.
The Woman Who Was Always Marrying, Always Divorcing.
She is the Owner of the Sea.

She is – Don't name her.
Say simply *the one down there.*

She is the Owner of the Sea.

Father and daughter

My first words were an order.
I tugged off a mitten with my teeth, let it drop.
I reached up, commanded: "Hold!

Hold my hand!" He laughed, but shed a mitt, too.

He took my tiny fingers in his fist.
We walked slowly, claiming the ice –
risking frostbite, he'd brag, for love.

She keeps saying No

Nobody is good enough.
She halts each handpicked man
with her own upheld hand,
will not be wedded.

At each affront her father cowers
but he won't cringe forever –
the name of Shame's hot-headed little brother
is Rage.

Punch, stroke, caress

Once I'd punched the last slow thaw of a man
my own father had forced on me
I took a dog thank you for a companion.

I borrowed now and then a young husband
to train up in the trick of touch.

Difficult hair

She is beautiful
but spends too much time alone –
to comb, she says, her difficult hair.
She's far too close to her frisky dog,
she even calls it Husband.

Famine

We'll be punished for this.
It's no coincidence our fish, lately,
have been smaller, if any are caught at all.

Husband and I

Husband and I have our small island.

When provisions are low
he swims back to the mainland,
collects a parcel from my father.

He returns, head up,
gripping the heavy packet in his jaws
to keep it dry.

He waits until he's close to me
then he shakes all the water off himself,
the ruffian, and we both laugh.

Husband and I

Husband lays with me
again and again.

Famine

We are being punished for this.

When was the last time anyone saw a fish
longer than a spear-head?

Giant

Already I am a giant.

There must be whole nations
growing in my womb.

Pups

Eight pups: each is dog and each is human,
or they are the beginning of something new.

Pups

Eight sets of pups need more than breast milk.
Husband makes daily trips to my father, requesting meat.

A fatherly visit

"Why the need for so much meat?
Doesn't she know food is scarce?

Is she ill? Has she a real man, now,
as well as that self-satisfied dog!
I thought I would make a fatherly visit.

As I landed on the island
she was in the distance.

Before I was out of the kayak
a pack of young dogs ran up to me

wagging their tails and yelping, 'Grandad!'"

"Slut"

"Slut isn't the half of what they call her,
my own daughter, and she deserves all the
names."

Birthday present

"Almost a year passes and perhaps they think
I have forgotten the outrage, the disgrace.

When the dog comes to me for provisions
I place a large wrapped rock in the packet.

I tie it to his back, explaining it's precious,
a birthday present for them all."

Strong current

There is a strong current
between here and your father's,
Husband had told me.

I believe his death was that and simply age,
oh and the burden of so many repeated journeys.

On the day before his children's birthday
he died providing for his family.

I saw him, struggling, as if weighed down
yet not even a parcel in his jaws,

and then I saw nothing at all.

Taunt

My father arrives the following day.
It was meant to have been a celebration.

A shame your 'husband' failed to deliver
my little birthday present for all the 'family'.

Then I knew he had killed him.

Not safe for the nations

It is not safe for the nations.
From three pairs of shoes I have fashioned three flotillas.

I am only sorry I cannot send my children
to the safety of the moon.

A straw for each mast

I use a straw for each mast and with a word all the craft are full-size.

The oldest set of children I teach to build stone houses
and then set them off.

These are the first true people.

The next set of children I equip with bow and arrow
and then set them off.

These are the people who live in the South, our difficult neighbours.

The third set of children I teach to be expert traders, expert sailors, and then I set them off.

These are the people of the West, who always look ill.

The last set of children run up to me
crying, there are no more ships!
Please, mother, keep us safe, too!

You will be safe.
You will be unseen.

These are the invisible people.

Return

I return to my father.

Look, he says, as if nothing had happened,
there is a man here, out of the ordinary.

He's already brought gifts of fish
sharing them with everybody.

He is tall and not from anywhere near here –
he has come from over the sea.

He seeks your hand in marriage.

"Hand." For a second I look at my hands
but I humour my father.

Seduced

The right song disguises any creature.
When he sang he was a man to me,
more than any local boy.

Reaching in

You may not see my face, he says,
but please, touch my hair.

I reach in, beneath his hood.

My fingers touch. His hair
is soft as down.

Crossing the ocean

I was between sleeping and waking,
ocean and cloud. I was flying.

My arms encircled him –
I clasped my fingers together, held fast.

That morning

I woke to the stink of fish breath.
My lover is a bird-spirit, a fulmar:
a short-arse – half albatross, half gull.

Alone

I do not love him,
but I miss him.

He stays out days
to bring the best back for me,
but fish is fish is fish.

Sometimes

Sometimes I sing to myself?

I imagine my father hearing me,
locating sorrow from a song –

finding me, leading me to safety, taking my hand,
and teaching my abductor a lesson or two.

In the distance

Here he is, finally,
my father –

not a day, not a week,
but a year later,
persuading the waves,
please, if you will,

make way for me.

Not lover

[two miscarriages

[make way for me
my lover had said
and I
made way for him

[not lover, captor]

Father, assassin

He scales the cliff easily.

Since he grips his beloved fish-knife
between his teeth
he has the appearance of smiling.

Rage in grief

When they discovered the murdered bird-spirit
it wasn't the storm his friends called down on us
that made escape
          impossible
it was the song they sing to this day:
rage in grief.

First to break

My father was the first to break,
pleading like a seabird himself,
Have the girl! Have the girl!

(Please,
let the waves
equalise us in loss.)

He bundled me,
flailing, choking,

into the blue.

Grip

I believed I was not made to sink.
I bobbed up, found the kayak, and gripped.

The fingers

She won't let go.

I hack at the tips of her fingers
with the fish-knife her mother gave me.

The scraps of flesh drop –
                                  Seals bob up!
and still my daughter holds on.

She won't let go.

I hack down to the knuckles
with the fish-knife her mother once gave me.
The scraps of flesh drop –
                    Walruses bob up!
and still my daughter holds on.

She. will. not. let. go.

I hack down to the last joints
with that blunt old fish-knife her mother once gave me.
The scraps of flesh drop –
                    Whales bob up!
My daughter's hands are just stumps.

She sinks.

Welcoming party

When my father finally reached land he was emaciated
but the dogs who found him still found a little meat.

Unusually for wild creatures they didn't kill him straightaway.
They seemed almost human.

They started with his balls and then his prick
and then gave tender loving care

to his fingers: biting, cracking, then chewing them, one by one.

You will have to visit me

You will have to visit me
if you want plenty.

In my new home underwater
my hair easily tangles

and these likenesses
of seal and walrus and whale

are not clasps or hair clips,
they are spirits, caught up in the snags.

I have no fingers to clear them.

You will have to visit me
if you want plenty.

Send me
a hunter, a powerful singer

who will jab me, make me bleed,
but comb my hair softly,

who will release all the animals

with the gentle strength of song.

THE OLD WOMAN WHO CHANGED HERSELF
INTO A MAN

Winter

It's the season the families move on from us.
There are no caribou here in winter.

They leave us, an old woman and a young woman,
knowing there is little to live on this far from the world.

Stone house

Ours is a stone house so perhaps the first people made it.

Questions

Is it right for a woman to sew the hide of a caribou,
but wrong to spear one?

Is it right for a woman to butcher a seal,
but wrong to harpoon one?

Is it right for a woman to cook a char,
but wrong to hook it?

There are fewer rules here
when the hunting families have moved on.

'Adopted daughter'

I am a very old woman now.

I was 'quite old' when she came to me. She was an orphan.

They call her my adopted daughter, and the term is useful enough.

Transformed

I will marry the girl, I will be a man.

I cut off my toes and they sniff and bark.
They wag their tails, they are my dogs.

I cut off my right nipple and it's sharp, a spear.

I cut off my left nipple and it's sharp too, a harpoon.

I make a harpoon rope from the hair on my head,
fishing line from the finer hairs lower down.

I cut out the place between my legs and I have the sledge we need.

I am a man, ready to hunt, ready to marry.

Learning

My husband caught her first seal at the lampside.
It smelt strongly of pee so she gave it to the dogs.

Even they thought twice about it. And they used to be toes!

I went to bed with my husband, hungry.

My husband caught his second seal at the doorway.
It smelt almost as bad as the first one so she gave it to the dogs.

They ate it quickly, though they grumbled about it.

I went to bed with my husband, hungry.

My husband caught his third seal at the porch.
It didn't smell so bad but we couldn't stomach it.

The dogs fought over it.

I went to bed with my husband, nigh on starving.

The fourth seal was caught on the ground-ice
and it was good meat.

I don't know why we couldn't eat it.

The dogs shared it among themselves.
Though we went to our bed empty we felt optimistic.

My husband caught his fifth seal way out on the sea-ice.
He got there thanks to his dogs and his sledge.

The meat was good and to be honest that way of hunting
set the pattern for our whole way of life.

Arrival

She was a man now
and that explains my baby.

More questions

Sometimes my husband
would hunt without the sledge and dogs.

It was Spring and our stone house
had its first visitor while my husband was away.

"Whose dogs are these?" the man asked,
knowing they couldn't be mine.

"My foster mother's," I said, plainly.

"Whose sledge is this?" the man asked,
giving me a look I didn't want to return.

"My foster mother's," I said.

"Who has caught these seals?"
"I think you know who."

Confession

I told him our history.

I had just finished when the dogs outside started kicking up a fuss.

A man's voice greeted them, my husband's,
but I knew another change was taking place.

Return

I am an old woman again.
At the house door I saw my wife had a visitor.
I saw there was a man inside the stone house.
I was ashamed and I was frail again, an old woman.
Help, I called out to my daughter, Help.

She came to me and led me in.
The visitor greeted me respectfully but did not linger.
He is the reason you and everyone else knows our story.

KIVIUQ

I

THE BOY AND THE STORM

Have you seen Kiviuq?

Have you seen Kiviuq?

I heard he moved to the far south.
I heard he followed the birds when they flew to the
summer lands.
I heard he settled at the shore where the seas don't freeze.

Greenland and Iceland would be stepping stones to
Kiviuq!
Maybe he is living beyond the second step, in Scotland?

I heard he is slowly becoming stone. Lichen has settled on
his face
and these days he doesn't like to be among people.

Have you seen Kiviuq? Is his story coming to an end?

An orphan

My grandmother was an angakkuk
but even shape-shifters, travellers in the spirit world,
even healers need a helper. They need company.

I was given to my grandmother, a trade maybe.
I know I was an orphan.

Our neighbour

Kiviuq was our neighbour then, a young man.
He wasn't mean – unlike certain other boys.

"Leave him alone, he's half your size!"
he told my tormentors
but they were quick to reply:

"Keep that big opening in your face shut –
or we'll shut it up for you, with blood."

What my grandmother told me about Kiviuq

His father had been one of the tuutaliit –
a half-seal, a selkie, a merman of a kind.
You'll have a word for it in your language?

He would help the hunters.

Where seals claw out a breathing hole in the sea-ice
hunters wait by the opening.
A seal comes up for air and then the hunter has him.

(Never forget, melt some snow so the dead seal's spirit can drink.)

Under the ice

One day Kiviuq's father was under the ice.
He found a handsome seal for the men
and chased it towards the surface.
The seal was lithe and he was clever:
he dodged the harpoon that lay in wait.
Some say the hunter at the breathing hole
was jealous of the seal-man.
Kiviuq's father was harpooned in the seal's wake
and the breathing hole filled with blood.

(Never forget, melt some snow so the dead seal's spirit can drink.)

I don't want to

Grandmother, I don't want to go out of the snowhouse.

I'm not the strongest of boys.
I already have rips in my hood where the gang has torn at my parka.
I already have bruises where the gang's stones have hit me.
I have cuts where the gang's sticks have jabbed me.

Do you want me to lose an eye?

Grandmother loses patience

My grandmother sent me out anyway
and I collected another rip in my hood for her.

My grandmother sent me out anyway
and I collected another bruise for her.

My grandmother sent me out anyway
and look here's another cut for you.

My grandmother sent me out anyway
and I refused.

When darkness falls, she said,
kill me a baby seal.

Baby seal

I waited for darkness.
I slipped out of the snowhouse.
I made my way to the sea ice and I found a baby seal.

With the harpoon my father had given my grandmother for safe-keeping
I killed the baby seal.

It took more than one jab and less than seven.

Important question

'Did you drip melted snow in the seal's mouth
to quench the spirit's thirst?'

Yes, grandmother.

Skinning

'You should have used a club,
you have damaged the skin.'

'You should have used a club
the seal felt more pain than is right.'

Since my grandmother was an angakkuk
she repaired the cuts.

Since my grandmother was an angakkuk
she stripped the baby seal of its skin in no time.

Since my grandmother was an angakkuk
she stripped the baby seal without a single rip.

She took care to cut round the eyes.
Even the eyeholes kept their delicate shape.

The skin suit

Put the seal suit on, she said, and I put the seal suit on.
A very good fit.

You already had seal-like eyes. You take after your father.
The disguise is perfect.

As this is your first seal we should have a celebration
but there are one or two tasks to complete before then.

Jeopardy

Do you recognise me, grandmother?
Don't mistake me for a seal and kill me!

Women don't hunt, now do they?
I will always recognise you.

(Of course women hunt
but my grandmother knew that.)

Puddle

Now, do you know in the dripping part of our home,
there is a puddle?

I know it.
(How could I not know it,

my grandmother had been training me
to hold my breath in its water for months –

for so long that the white pelt of the seal I wear
is now out of season.)

Will you dive into it, my seal-boy?

I made no reply. I dived into it.

Surface

A little later, swimming from one hole in the universe to another
I surfaced. I was in a puddle on the other side of the settlement.

Bait

I am my own bait.
I am a seal walking through the settlement.

The boys who gave me their presents
of bruises and cuts begin to follow.

Kiviuq is there and like any person he would like to kill a seal.
Or does he understand a white seal at this time of year
must mean enchantment.

All run after me.

Since seals seldom win running contests
I only just make it to the sea edge in time.

The hunt

They are in their kayaks but when I'm a seal I'm a good swimmer.

They are in their kayaks but now I'm feeling more human than seal.

They are in their kayaks surrounding me and their harpoons are poised.

Grandmother!

Amauti, the large-hooded parka

If it was right and I was strong enough
I would still carry that boy on my back.
If it was right and I was strong enough
I would still carry that boy within my parka.

He'd peep out from our hood proud as an owl
resting on an ancient inuksuk, this cairn of me.

The storm

Grandmother! I heard
and I saw the threat to him.

Not a simple task to fashion a storm. Not a simple task to direct it.

Not a simple task to overturn the kayak of the cruellest boy.
Not a simple task to overturn the kayak of the jeering sidekick.
Not a simple task to overturn the kayak of the quiet boy
                    who 'just went along with it'.

Let them drown then.

And spare the good neighbour.

Saved

The next day there was many a seal closer to the settlement.
They had come in to shelter. Though most men searched for the children
some readied their nets and clubs. I saw one man about to strike a young seal.

Leave him, I cried out, can't you see he's my grandson?
The boy pulled off the seal-skin and the hunter saw it was true.
They found the bodies of the boys a little further down the beach.

2

AFTER THE STORM

Kiviuq on the open sea

When the storm cleared Kiviuq was alone in his kayak.
He paddled all that day but there was no land to be seen.

He paddled a second day and he saw a darkness ahead,
maybe it was land, no, it was just dark water.

On the third day he saw a lightness ahead,
and it was shallow water, a hint of land.

A snow bunting settled on the prow.
Where the sea's cloth billowed and finished Kiviuq saw a beach.

First Voices

He was exhausted but he dragged his kayak away from the water.

He heard a voice crying out, "Please,
clean my eye!" and Kiviuq went to find out.

A seal-bone was there on the beach, all mucky –
"Please, please clean my eye!" it whimpered –

and Kiviuq cleaned away the dirt.
There was a small hole near one end. Thank you, said the bone.

Kiviuq saw it was the 'dog' in the children's game.
Playing with his brothers, he always hoped to get a turn of it.

Then Kiviuq heard a voice crying out, "Please,
I am drowning!" and Kiviuq went to find out.

A lemming was struggling to swim in a rock pool
although it could easily have stood up in the shallow water.

Kiviuq picked it out of the pool and set it on dry land.
Thank you, said the lemming, that ocean was about to finish me.

Kiviuq's exhaustion finally hit him.
He just managed to take his boots off and his outer clothes
to dry them in the sun, and then he succumbed to sleep.

Voices

In his dreams a friendly woman's voice wakes him three times.

The first time the voice warns him the tide has come up to his kayak.
He wakes and there is no one there. He draws the kayak up beyond the beach.

The second time the voice warns him the sun can't dry his boots thoroughly.
He wakes and there is no one there. He turns the boots to fully catch the sun.

The third time he wakes the voice says there is a home here for you
and the woman who belongs to that voice is there right in front of him.

He gathers all his things and follows her to her home.

A welcome

She offered her drying rack for his clothes and for his boots,
and a bed for a proper rest.

The drying rack

Awake after the deepest sleep Kiviuq finds the woman cooking.
But he is having one or two problems. He tells her:

No offence, but your drying rack backs away when I try to retrieve my clothes.
A pair of tongs comes out from under the bed snapping at me
when I try to retrieve my boots.

No offence, she replies,
but I put your clothes on the drying rack and your boots,
so it's your turn to fetch them.

Kiviuq is surprised at this turn in the conversation.
He summons a polar bear to his side.
Kiviuq suggests to the woman she might modify her opinion.

Kiviuq gathers his things with her blessing, if that's what that look was.
Now let me leave, he says, seeing the doorway is much narrower than before.

I let you in, she says, you can let yourself out.
Kiviuq signals and the polar bear roars. The doorway widens again.

Now Kiviuq is outside, running with all his things in his arms.
The polar bear's vanished, job done it must have thought.

Watch out for the mussels, says the seal-bone with the eye.
Trip on a bunch of shells?, Kiviuq thinks, Thanks for the warning,
but isn't that on the over-protective side?

Then he sees mussels the size of men approaching at a rate of knots
and they're looking peckish. Kiviuq gives them a body-swerve just in time.
He escapes to his kayak but the woman has made the sea rough.

She calls out to him: "why are you leaving so quickly?
I thought we had a Relationship! And do you have to be so happy about it?
Can't you see I'm still grieving for the loss of all we had together?"

She brandishes her ulu (that's the crescent-shaped blade a woman uses).
She shouts over to him, I could have sliced you up with this!

Kiviuq brandishes his harpoon.
He shouts back at her: I could have speared you with this!
She is affronted, hurt, she starts to sob in anger.

Kiviuq paddles faster and the sea becomes calmer.
Soon he can't see the figure of the woman crying, crouched on a rock.

3

THE SPIDERS AND THE BEADS

Where spiders make beads

There's an island where tiny spiders make glass beads as fine as dew
and with delicate thread and stitching embroider clothes with them.

Kiviuq landed there and before long right in front of their eyes
he took string after string of the beads and a beautiful embroidered jacket.

They cried as he left and their tears looked like their own see-through beads.
They had liked him, they had wanted him to stay when they first saw him.

Strangers

The snow bunting wakes Kiviuq: we've got company.
Two men in kayaks come alongside and guide him to shore.

At a meat cache they share caribou and start talking.
The men it seems grew up on the same shore as Kiviuq.

"It's years since I've been there. I'm an old man now!" laughs Kiviuq.
As he opens his mouth one of the men sees the unique shape of his teeth.

"Father! Those teeth can only belong to my father!
Look! We are your sons!"

Homecoming

Kiviuq's sons travel just ahead of him to tell his parents
he has survived. He is well. He is returning.

They meet their grandfather at the shore
He is one of the few men left in the village.
He had been preparing to hunt for seal but he is frail now.
It's years since he has brought home anything more
than stories of the one that got away.

He is overwhelmed by his grandsons' news:
he has been waiting for so long to hear that Kiviuq is alive.
Incomplete grief – extravagant hope – have become his life.
He listens twice to his grandsons before he understands and then
before Kiviuq can land, the knowledge strikes him dead.

Their grandmother has been waiting for so long to hear that Kiviuq is alive.
Looking out to sea all that time for the first sign of his return,
she has worn footprints into the rock she has been standing upon.
She listens twice to her grandsons before she understands and then,
before Kiviuq can land, the knowledge strikes her dead.

Kiviuq's wives

"Aasiggai, aasiggai, aasi, aasi, aasiggai. Here I am!" sings Kiviuq
as he paddles his kayak within earshot of his old village.
No one else has a song like that! All the women come down to the shore.
The village has declined since Kiviuq was taken away by the storm.
There are very few men here.

Kiviuq's two wives walk down to the shore to welcome him home.

One had married since his disappearance
and, together, the new husband-and-wife had flourished.
She looks well. She's one of the few in the settlement who doesn't look
    drawn.
She has handsome clothes and smiles a complicated smile when she meets
    Kiviuq.
Kiviuq kills her husband.

[Kiviuq kills her husband – thinking, How could she! –
or he spares him, thinking with practical kindness,
What was his wife supposed to do?
One story overlays another, there is no resolution.]

Kiviuq's other wife had remained alone since his disappearance
and is gaunt. Kiviuq recognises the clothes she is wearing.
They're stitched-together scraps from clothes she and the children used to
    wear.
"Here I am!" Kiviuq had sung and she has a song in reply:
"I have been waiting.! My vagina has been idle,
I assure you it has received no comings-and-goings!
My vagina has been closed to any man.
Now you are back, believe me, it's wide open for you!"

Kiviuq gives all the women the beads the spiders had made.
To the wife who had remained solitary he gives nothing,
there's a pause, and then he gives her the embroidered jacket.

4

SMOKE, OR IS IT STEAM?
Iguttaqjuaq, the Bee Woman

Another shore

Kiviuq is out on the open water again.

While he paddles he remembers meeting another woman
a long time before all this began.

He had landed on another shore and straightaway there's a house.
Something not right with it. Tumbledown, no roof,

but smoke or is it steam coming out the top.
It was both – that's the smell of meat cooking –
but what meat, Kiviuq couldn't place it.

Maybe a welcome

Well, meat's meat, maybe there's a welcome here.

Shadows

Kiviuq passes a window, casting a shadow into the house.
There's a large old woman bumbling about indoors.

She's placing skins on her drying rack and now she's cooking.
"Oh, clouds!" she says, "I wasn't expecting that," meaning Kiviuq's shadow.

"I'll need to get busy." She gives the pot a vigorous stir.

Is that rain?

Kiviuq climbs up the house wall and looks down.
He now sees what kind of skins are stretched out on the drying rack –
human skins.

Is she a spirit? They say you can tell by looking at the eyes.
She's directly beneath him so he lands a gob of spit
right in the centre of her head. But she doesn't look up.

"Oh, rain!" she says, "I wasn't expecting that.
I didn't know I had a leak in my roof."

Now she does look but can't see anything because of her bushy eyebrows.
She stretches one eyebrow out, cuts it off and puts it into the pot.
She does exactly the same with the other one.
Then she looks directly up at Kiviuq.

What just happened?

Did he just lose his footing, did he faint?

It feels like months not minutes.
Did he actually die?

He wakes up in the old woman's bed.

A kind of welcome

"Hello," said the woman. "A human!
Welcome, rest you, the weather can only get worse.
It's clouding over and there have been a few spots of rain."

Kiviuq saw some human eyeballs in the stew, and a hand.
Two eyebrows bobbed up now and then as she stirred the pot.

"I've taken your wet things off. Lie down, there's no need to get up,"
the old woman said in a sing-song voice, almost humming.

Kiviuq saw that he was on a narrow bunk, edged with human skulls.
He saw his parka and boots on the rack.

"Now I just have to visit the heather before the downpour.
Make yourself at home while I'm gone."

She puts on a thick fur coat which has bands of black and yellow.
Then she practically flies out of the house.

A word in your ear

The second the woman buzzes away
one of the skulls starts to speak –
"Get out of here as soon as you can!
You'll end up like us if you're not careful."

Kiviuq recognises the voice – it's one of his brothers.
"We all ended up in the pot," says another skull.
"She said I was delicious," he says proudly,
though he adds: "Not that that's a consolation."

Kiviuq puts his boots and his parka back on.
The drying rack twitches at this touch but it is just a twitch.
He runs back to his kayak and the snow bunting
and tries to make his escape.

A proposal

"Marry me, Kiviuq!" says the Bee Woman, calling from the shore.
"You are a powerful angakkuk, Sir, and in case you hadn't noticed,
I am too! We would be the perfect match!"

"That's a kind offer, but you know you're just not my type.
Thank you for the golden time we shared together but I think you know
we're just not compatible. It's not you, it's me!"

The bee woman is furious and dashes her ulu against a boulder in the sea
and the blade shatters.

The whole sea seems to freeze over, the first time sea ice has ever been seen.

Kiviuq is dismayed but the snow bunting knows how to pick a way through.

5

DRIFTWOOD, NEEDLE AND THREAD

Mother and daughter

The next home Kiviuq came to there was a middle-aged woman
and her grown-up daughter.

They were both wolves in the form of humans.

"Hello!" the women said to him, brightly,
at exactly the same time.

"Please do stay – you're most welcome!"
They said that together, too.

They showed Kiviuq their sleeping quarters. "We all share, here," they said.

Wood

Right in the middle of the bunk was a long length of driftwood.
It had smooth twisted branches which stuck out like arms and legs.
Kiviuq couldn't help noticing there was one shorter thick branch
where a penis on a man would be. It was sticking up,
you could've hung a parka on it.

It was then that it crossed Kiviuq's mind
there was a certain scent in this part of the home
and he couldn't quite place it. No, wait, it was at least two aromas –
the first was fresh sperm, though with a pine-fresh addition.
And the second was musky. Yes, a vagina's scent,
the scent of the juices which are set free when a woman is enjoying having sex.

Useful driftwood

It was still morning so Kiviuq offered to hunt.
No need, the women said.

They dragged the driftwood down to the shore
and sure enough in no time he'd caught two seals for them.

"So, he's your husband?" Kiviuq said, and "Yes," the older woman replied.
She looked at her daughter and after a pause she said "Yes," too.

The young woman was strong. She carried the carcasses
and the older woman dragged the driftwood
and the procession quickly made its way home.

Grumbles

That night Kiviuq went to bed with the older woman
and – right in the middle of having sex – the driftwood started
    grumbling.
Kiviuq pulled out and mother said, oh
don't mind that lump of wood. But Kiviuq moved over to the daughter.
She was glad to see Kiviuq pay her a visit.
Right in the middle of having sex
the driftwood started the same old grumble routine.
It was even louder than the first time, and Kiviuq
pulled out. The daughter said, oh
don't mind that twig. But Kiviuq spat at the driftwood,
another juice to add to its layers of polish.
Mr Driftwood fell silent and Kiviuq and daughter,
like the drill and bow used for starting a fire, went back to their kindling.

Mittens and beads

The driftwood was up and out early the next morning.
Kiviuq saw him swimming south and that was the last time anyone saw him.

Kiviuq started to make a life for himself there.
He'd hunt and the women would butcher the creatures and cook.

They'd even make mittens for him, and give him beads.
He'd pretend he'd lost them but really stow them in the front of his kayak.
They always made him more.

He admired the young woman and he married her.
Life's perfect after a wedding, right?

Needle

Mother and daughter were alone together.

"Wait a second," said the mother,
"I've just seen something jumping around in your hair!"

"Get it off me, mother! What will Kiviuq think
if he finds lice setting up home in my hair!"

The mother had a closer look,
parting her daughter's hair with her fingers.

"I can't see anything yet," she said. "Keep looking!"
She gently pulled her daughter's hair back to make a pony-tail.

Then she took a long needle
and pushed it into her daughter's ear, right into the brain.

You don't survive that.

Thread

The mother skinned her daughter's body
and where she'd had to make a cut or two she re-stitched it with sinews.

She dressed herself in her daughter, from foot to face.
As her daughter had been taller than she was
she had to gather in some of the skin and clip it around the hips.

"Not a perfect fit," she said to herself,
"But men – you know – they don't have a clue."

Kiviuq at the shore

"You're struggling, today," Kiviuq said. "Are you well?"
"Never better," said the woman, but she couldn't lift the seal.

"Where's your mother?" Kiviuq said.
"Visiting family. One of her relatives has died – completely out of the blue."

"There's something different about you. Do you want me to tell you what it is?"
"Tell away. I love it when my husband pays me some attention."

"The skin of your daughter is gathered and clipped around your hips."

For the mother's sake

Kiviuq stayed in that place for a little longer.
He'd hunt and collect more mittens and beads.
They'd fuck with the mother wearing her daughter's skin
and sometimes, for the mother's sake, they'd fuck with it off.
The daughter was dead so Kiviuq was dead, what did it matter.

You're going to leave me, aren't you? the mother said.
Never, Kiviuq replied.

Mittens and beads

Here is Kiviuq in his kayak, loaded with mittens and beads,
and the snow bunting is his lookout.

They are travelling away from that place and that woman
through night and day.

6

IF YOU CAN'T BE GOOD BE CAREFUL

Stones and shells

Just as Kiviuq was approaching another remote house
a lemming crossed his path.

Kiviuq saw it was the one he'd rescued from a rock pool oh an age ago.

"Listen, Kiviuq," said the lemming without even saying hello.
"You saved my life once and now I'm going to save yours."

"When you lie down to sleep tonight make sure to protect your vitals.
There are large shells here and flat stones – place them over your body

but conceal them under your clothes. If you do, you might just
survive tonight." Kiviuq thanked the lemming who disappeared in a hurry.

What are my vitals, Kivuq asked himself,
before scooping up half the rocky beach. Then he walked up to the house.

Tails

There were two sisters in the house
and they were of a kind that's relatively rare these days:
they had scales from the midriff down and their bodies ended with a sharp
  tail.

They welcomed Kiviuq – "Be our guest" –
and he spent a happy enough evening with them.
When it came to bedtime he settled down on a bunk and pretended to go to
  sleep.

They started to talk about Kiviuq as if he would be a tasty piece of meat.
They wondered what tools and clothes they'd make from his bones and his
  skin.

A conversation between sisters

The sisters turned to another subject that interested them:
which of the women should get to kill Kiviuq.

"My tail is sharper than yours, sister," said the older woman,
"He won't know he's been attacked before it's too late."

"I like the pleasure of jabbing a man," said the younger sister,
"a tail should not be too sharp or it's all over too quickly."

The first sister had to agree. She wanted to see Kiviuq writhe
with her sister on top of him, jabbing him in every tender part.

"Well, sharpen your tail a little," she said, "We're not monsters."

On top

The younger woman clambered on top of Kiviuq
who was still pretending to be asleep.
Now, as if neither sleeping nor completely awake
but in that state of perception
when a person is aware of their lover
kissing and caressing them into full consciousness,
rousing them tenderly, humorously, to have sex,
Kiviuq mumbled, "Be my guest."

The woman's large tail was now tensed and raised up
and she held it there prolonging the moment, enjoying the tension.
Her sister looked on, taking pleasure in it all, too.
Finally the woman brought the arrow-end of her tail right down on Kiviuq,
full-force.

Flat stone

As her tail hit the flat stone concealed beneath Kiviuq's clothes
the woman shrieked in pain.
The shudder reverberated all the way back to her heart.
She was dead in the time it would have taken to say 'broken harpoon'.

Her sister backed away from Kiviuq and begged him to spare her.
"How could we know you were a powerful angakkuk?
Mermaids have to eat, too! We could survive on the usual,
on cod and on blubber – scavenged from carcasses we find on the beach –
but everyone needs variety in their diet, and refinement!
for their body, for their mind."

Kiviuq spared the older sister but he felt ill at ease in her house.
He didn't wait for morning to bid her farewell.

7

GRIZZLY

Turning away from the sea

Kiviuq had had enough of the sea and sea people.
He decided to trek further inland.

Further further further.
When he saw an inukshuk waiting for him
he knew he was in a new zone of being.
(An inukshuk is a cairn, built, in a certain light,
 in the likeness of a human.).

The inukshuk said nothing.

Kiviuq nodded and Kiviuq kept on walking.

Arguments

Before long he came to a settlement whose people were hungry,
they were arguing amongst themselves and were then suspicious of
    Kiviuq.
"Our meat cache keeps on getting raided. No-one knows who it is
so everyone thinks it's each other. But wait, mister, you look well fed."

"I'm no thief. Bury me beneath the meat cache
and I'll find you your meat criminal," Kiviuq told them.

Inside the meat cache

Beneath a pile of frozen raw meat and rocks on top of all that
Kiviuq became frozen himself. If he had a pulse you couldn't have felt it.

Was he alive?
He was alive alright and it wasn't long before his plan started to work.

He heard the heavy tread of a grizzly bear approaching.
Rocks which had taken two men to place on top of the meat cache were
  flicked off.

A large bear was there, tucking into the meat, gnash gnash gnash
working down the pile.

Only a man

When it got to Kiviuq the bear said out loud, "Only a man,
but I could take it back in case we run out of everything else."

The bear was suspicious. There hadn't been cannibals in the region for years,
was this some kind of trick?

It sniffed Kiviuq's nose and mouth to see if he was breathing,
but Kiviuq could breathe out of his backside and that's what he did.

Then the bear sniffed Kiviuq's backside –
Kiviuq switched holes and breathed out of his nose.

Family man

The bear decided it was time to share the last of the meat with his family.
It dragged Kiviuq for a little while, pulling him along as if he were a sledge.

He even put the last thing left from the meat cache on to Kiviuq's stomach,
the leg of a caribou.

As he was being dragged, Kiviuq began to thaw.
If you had placed your fingers on his neck you would have felt a pulse.

Kiviuq held on now and again to saplings and low-hanging branches,
slowing the bear down and tiring him.

Whenever the bear turned round Kiviuq had let go and looked like a corpse.
The bear sniffed Kiviuq's face, the bear sniffed his backside, nothing.

There's a faster way, thought the bear,
thinking it was Kiviuq's awkward body which was slowing everything down.

So the bear took his bearskin off and he was just a man.

He humped Kiviuq and the caribou leg onto the bearskin
and made a travois for his treasure.

Kiviuq stopped playing his snagging trick.
Dragging Kiviuq and the caribou leg, the man-bear began to move quickly.

Napping

Finally the bear arrived home and was greeted by his two sons.

"What a find!" they told him, meaning the caribou. "Oh, it was nothing. Children, help yourself, but remember to share."

The bear cubs settled down to eat the caribou. Their father put his skin back on. Exhausted by dragging Kiviuq, he settled down to nap.

Kiviuq opened his eyes just for a second and saw an axe within reach.

Wake up, Dad

"Father, I saw the man's eyes open and shut."
"Don't bother me now, I am trying to sleep."

"Father, I think I can see him breathing."
"Seriously, boys, I need to rest."

"Father, he is standing right over you, please!"
Kiviuq cut Daddy Bear's leg off with one sweep of the axe.

The bear's wife

Kiviuq hadn't reckoned with the bear's wife.
She appeared when she heard the cubs crying.

She was in human form at that point –
she had just walked in from lighting a fire at the back.

Like her husband she could switch between human and
      animal
and when she saw Kiviuq and what he had done

she thought he had killed her husband.

Kill a bear, a bear kills you.
She paused to put her bearskin on.

Running

While the she-bear was getting ready to go out for the evening
Kiviuq ran as fast as he could. He knew bears run faster than men.

When he looked back she was already gaining on him.
Kiviuq dribbled a necklace of saliva into his hand.

He wrapped the beads of spit round a small mound of earth.
"Be a mountain!" he said and the mound was a mountain.

Kiviuq thought putting a mountain in the bear's way
would be enough to keep him safe.

He slowed down, caught his breath.
But he might as well look back. Better safe than sorry?

He did look back – and saw the bear was on his side of the mountain,
moving fast, head down, close.

Kiviuq had just come up to a small stream, which he stepped over.
Again he trickled saliva onto his hand.

He drew one wet finger along the bank of the stream.
"Be a river!" he said, and the stream was a river.

This time he waited for the bear and she wasn't long in arriving.
When she saw the river she saw how broad and fast it was and she stopped.

How did you manage to cross the river! she cried out, exasperated.
It wasn't meant as a question but Kiviuq gave her an answer.

I kissed it. I licked it. I drank it, and then I could walk right across.
Oho, said the bear, and she got down into the river.

She kissed it. She licked it. She drank it, and she almost made it right across.

(When she kissed it
did she remember the kisses she once shared with her husband?
When she licked it
did she remember the licks her cubs used to give her, the snuffles?
When she drank it
was she not also gulping down her rage, quenching vengeance on her husband,
quenching vengeance on her two cubs, who she believed no longer had a father?

She drank the river, but you cannot drink a river.
As the water filled her stomach the water heated up.
Her stomach grew and grew.
Kiviuq watched.
Her stomach grew and grew.
She was pregnant with anger.
Kiviuq watched.
Her stomach grew and grew
and then her stomach exploded.)

Fog was everywhere, in fact this was the way fog was first created,
and the bear lay there dead.

8

THE LAKE SPIRIT

'Marginal territory'

The fog cleared and that fog had been weather fog and it had been time fog.

Kiviuq's been living further inland for a few years,
'marginal territory', caribou if you're lucky, if you're skilled.
Luck and skill, you need both.

A new home

He has two wives
and in his mind, fine, they're not his first love, the driftwood's wife,
but they're hard workers. He's pretty and they're handsome.

They share the same turf house.
They're all good to each other, each to every one.

Kiviuq doesn't know it

He doesn't know it but one of his wives is an angakkuk.
He doesn't know it but the lake at the back of the house has a spirit living
    there.
He doesn't know it but the spirit has always helped them get through
    winter –
lake trout the length of an arm, caribou by the shore.
He doesn't know it, but the angakkuk and the spirit have worked together
to keep them all alive.

Sleeping

Why are the women so sleepy?
That's three times he's come back, caribou on his shoulder,
and seen them dozing. Barely half the firewood gathered.

The women talk by the lake

The angakkuk asks the younger woman
if she wants to call the spirit of the lake.
She doesn't feel worthy – "I'm no angakkuk!" –
but the older woman reassures her.

"I'll scatter the little stones, and you call him."

Summoned

The angakkuk gathers a handful of small stones.
She scatters them far across the surface of the lake as if they were seeds.
Each sends gentle ripples out and the ripples melt into each other like
     kindness.

The young woman looks at the angakkuk
and the angakukk's look says, Don't worry.

"Lake spirit," the other woman says, "I am waiting for you!
The mouth between my legs is hungry for your meat!"

Immediately, a large penis rises from the lake.

Apprentice

She learns so fast. She'll be a powerful angakkuk.
She's even placed her clothes on a rock away from the lake edge –
to avoid any wash!

In the shallows she chuckles affectionately to begin with,
then she uses her mouth and she uses her hand.

Then she straddles him, guides him.
She catches my eye but she knows she needs to concentrate.

To see her so near but 'far off', absorbed. Riding. And being ridden.
To see at the same time her fingers moving about herself,
dextrous seamstress, taking pleasure in all her skills.

When she wades back I see the blush across her throat and face.
I think of the ripples which spread across the lake when I scattered
    the stones.

Shivers

She dries me off, helps to dress me.

"We'll wait a little," she says.
"You know – a man can need a little rest...
at certain times."

We let the shivers fall away.

A question

Do you think he liked my silly joke?

"Joke?"

Mouth and meat?

"That is a joke and that is not a joke."

(Straight face, and then we both giggle.)

Again

In a short while I scatter the stones,
and my friend the angakkuk calls to the lake spirit.

"Lake spirit," she says, "I am here!
Are you rested? Are you ready?
Penis, rise! My vagina is ready for you!"

Firewood

The women wander back from the lake,
gathering a few pieces of firewood on their way home.
If the weather stays like this, who needs firewood!

They feel tired and as soon as they are inside they fall asleep.

Kiviuq the Hunter has seen everything.

Summoned a third time

At first Kiviuq skimmed a stone hard across the lake.
It cut across the water and sank.

Then he remembered the ritual and was more gentle:
he scattered a handful of stones and saw the little ripples.

"Lake spirit," he called softly. (Any hunter learns to mimic.), "I am here."
"I am waiting for you! Are you rested? Are you ready?
Rise, penis! My vagina is waiting for you!"

Taking it all in

When he saw the penis rise up from the lake again
Kiviuq took the bottom half of his clothes off and waded into the water.

He took hold of the upright cock carefully, caressed it, worked it.
He dribbled a little spit on it to make it more slippery.

He straddled it. He guided the large penis
into himself – with a catch of excitement at the soft 'barb'.

He was surprised his backside could take it all in.

Now he knew he had to concentrate. Riding. And being ridden.
At the same his fingers were on his own penis,
dextrous man.

Red

When the lake spirit had finished
Kiviuq turned round and sliced the lake spirit's penis off.
The lake filled with blood.

Kiviuq made sure to keep the penis.

As he waded back he created a viscose red wash
which lapped up over the rock where he'd placed his clothes.

I made the dinner tonight

He wakes the women.

"Why are your clothes all splashed with blood?" the older women asks.
While you were sleeping I made the dinner tonight, Kiviuq tells them.

I lit a fire to cook, though there is little firewood in the house.
(The women are silent.)

The younger woman says, "It smells rich. What is it?"
Taste it, both of you. Perhaps your mouth will recognise the texture
if not the flavour.

"It feels hard but also soft. It tastes of fish but also of meat,"
said the older woman. The younger woman was pale and silent,
she finally knew more about a subject than her teacher.

Kiviuq said, "It is the prick of your secret husband!"

Choose

The women are terrified but Kiviuq is determined.
Tell me, what are you most afraid of? –
Maggots, which eat the dead? Or fire, which eats the living?

"Fire," says the younger woman, whimpering,
and Kiviuq sets her on fire, watches her burn to death.

"Maggots," says the older women, the angakkuk. She does not look afraid.
Take the bottom half of your clothes off, Kiviuq says, and the angakkuk
    does it.

He opens his hand and it is full of maggots. They seethe on his palm.
He spreads them on the floor. Sit yourself down, he says, and she does.

She slips the bottom edge of her top beneath her for protection
but Kiviuq sees the manoeuvre and pulls it away. "Take your medicine."

Into every opening

The maggots move into every opening.
"My guts are dying," she tells him.

"My womb is dying," she tells him.
"My heart is dying," she tells him.

Finally the maggots come out through her mouth
and she says her last words: "I am dead."

She is only bones now.

A lemming is there between her ribs and it tries to escape
but he catches it and kills that creature, too – he sets it on fire.

It dies less than instantly.

He gathers the bodies of the women and buries them under two piles
of rocks.

9

THE FOX-WIFE

Not in that house

Kiviuq can't live in that house.
Hot anger, cold anger, atrocity.

But he needs to be close to the graves.
He sets a tent up nearby, lives basic.

Surviving

Years pass but they're a fog.
Kiviuq looks after himself, just.

Three meals

Kiviuq trudges back from a hunt, empty-handed.
What's strange, something's strange, something in the tent.

He's fully alive again, hunter. Creeps in. The scent,
faint. Hare?

A pot of hare stew is waiting for him.
He tastes it, careful. It's cold but that's fine, tastes good. So what if it's poison.

It's not poison.

Another hunt, another failure.
Kiviuq trudges back, bent down, bad luck across his shoulders,
heavier than a caribou.

The scent, a little stronger. Hare, certainly.
There's a fresh pot of hare stew. Lukewarm, ok, but this is no time to be
    choosy.
Tasty.

A third hopeless hunt, you get the pattern:
Kiviuq's starting to think no animals are left in the world.
(That'll never happen, right?)

But home again and there's a full, strong, rich, scent. Hare stew.
A pot of it is waiting for him. Piping hot, delicious.

From the grave

Kiviuq conceals himself behind a man
made of stones, the way-marker they call an inukshuk.

There is a movement among the rocks of the angakkuk's grave
and now a being in winter white
shyly, carefully, picks its path to the tent.

She's an arctic fox, dainty, strong.
Kiviuq could see himself wearing a scarf from that tail,
or fashioning muffled shoes from a length of her fur,

perfect for silent approaches.

Coat

I don't want him to know my nature yet.
He'll scent my fox skin if I wear it inside the tupik
so let's just clip it here to the guy-rope before I go in.

Inukshuk

The inukshuk has moved, closer.

She noticed only this moment,
but now she sees
it has moved a little each day.

It's Kiviuq, of course, hiding behind it, stalking her,
but she still leaves her fox skin on the rope before she goes in.

Snatched

Kiviuq holds up the fox skin and calls out to her:
"Fox! Come out of my tent, I've something you seem to have lost!"

The fox pulls the tent flap back and she is a naked woman.
She has long white hair and Kiviuq likes that.

He is dangling her fox skin just out of reach.
Give it back to me, she says firmly, shaking with shy indignation.

"What's it worth...lady?"

Eyes meeting eyes

Silence.
Eyes
                       meeting eyes.

She tries to snatch it back
but he's too quick.

She looks angrier than before.
Is she the angakkuk who Kiviuq killed,
reincarnated?

"Why are you living on top of that grave?"

Silence,
eyes meeting eyes.

This is what we are going to do, she says,
feeling courage grow within her.
You're going to
                    hand me back my pelt.

and I'm going to
marry you.

Silence. Eyes.

Lovingly

Kiviuq and his wife –
Does she have a name in this story? No.

Kiviuq and his wife share their lives lovingly
and if the fox-wife is the dead angakkuk he's happy,
she deserves a second life and don't ask
what Kiviuq deserves or if he's sorry. We're not in that kind of world,

are we?

Wolverine

Then they're away from the home, hunting together
and there's the low mound of a snow house ahead of them.
They're suspicious, you would be, and a wolverine
ambles out of the entrance, straightaway saying
Hello stranger, let's not fight, I believe I've a half-brother
of a half-sister of yours, and Kiviuq and the fox-wife
don't believe it but they're not going to ask for details,
Come on let me help you build yourselves a snow house
right next to mine for the warmth, we'd better be quick,
you know as well as I do summer's a memory of a memory,
look at that blizzard heading straight for us.

A new friend

Through the falling snow the wolverine
helps them build their own snow house,
turns out he's handy with his paws.

The fox-wife is in human form,
her fox-skin concealed in a parcel on the travois, packed tight.

They all work together
but the wolverine has the glad eye for the fox-wife.

When Kiviuq's not looking
the wolverine's sniffing her up and he's sniffing her down,

"Strong scent, lady!" he says,
"reminds me of something I can't quite put my finger on."

He opens his claws out like he wants to. She flinches.
She's angry and she's afraid. She moves away.

The final pieces

Now all three have to work together on the final pieces,
"You folks been married long?" the wolverine half-shouts,

"Seems like it to me," all nicey-nicey.
"Yes," they say together,

"We're a good – " Kiviuq starts to say.
"...team," she says,

and the couple smile at each other.

"Look at you," the wolverine grins,
"completing each other's sentences!"

A quiet moment

Later, inside the iglu – when Kiviuq's gone out to the travois –
suddenly the wolverine is all pally with the fox-wife again.

"Well this is nice and cosy," he tells her. He leans in with a gruff whisper:
"I'd like to complete your sentence."

Agreement

Now it's the fox-wife's turn to go out to bring things in.
Kiviuq and the wolverine are talking.

"Well, Hunter," the animal says, "we made a good snow home today.
The work that two fine males can achieve when they work together!"

"Not just us," Kiviuq corrects him, meaning the fox-wife.
The wolverine, says, "Right you are! Of course of course –

"With a little help from your fair lady, of course, heh heh heh."

Which reminds me

"Speaking of which, Kiviuq,
I don't think we've had a fair trade, have we?

I mean, think about it,
that blizzard would have flayed the two of you
if I hadn't helped you out. And if I hadn't lent you my iglu's wall
to build your own home against – well, you'd still be building your
    home now,
or you'd be two bodies inside a grave."

"I'm thinking, I'm just thinking," says the wolverine,
"now don't be taking any offence, there's a simple way of completing
    the trade."

Just as he said that the fox-woman came into view
entering the iglu loaded up with gear.
The wolverine looked at her with a glance
and Kiviuq knew what trade he was talking about.

"How about a wife exchange? Soon." the wolverine said
as if completing Kiviuq's thought.
"That would make things friendly, we'd be firmly family then."

The fox wife is looking pale and Kiviuq's looking at the ground
but neither can think of a way out of it, it's legitimate, it's tradition.

Bachelor?

"I didn't know you had a wife, wolverine?" Kiviuq says.

"Oh yes, quiet type, hard worker, sweet nature.
You'll see her tonight, for the swap."

Mrs Wolverine

The truth is the wolverine didn't have a wife.
For some reason, females tended to avoid him.
No problem, he said to himself, I'll just shit a wife.
He crouched down and he shat a human woman right out of his
      backside,
the biggest shite he'd shot out of his hind quarters
since he'd eaten a whole caribou a few years back
(now I come to think about, he said to himself,
a diseased beast I found in its death throes,
tastier than you'd expect, an acquired taste, I grant you, I'll give you that,
but I left barely a flake of flesh on the bone.")

He turned round and he finished shaping the shite into a woman,
finessed a bit of the detailing. But he didn't want to fuss for too long.
"Sure, one woman's the same as another,
Kiviuq's still gonna want to fuck that,
almost feel like having a go myself."

"But I better go, don't want to break my promise to the man,
time to visit next door."

House rules

Kiviuq and the wolverine meet at the entrance of the new iglu.

When I've left, Kiviuq tells him, seal the iglu from the inside.

Respect her.
Respect her shyness.
Don't sniff her.
When she gets up in the night for a pee, let her,
and don't go following her to watch.

Fire

Once inside, the wolverine started to seal the iglu,
rubbing snow into any gaps.

He wondered what the point of it all was.

Maybe the woman was sensitive to drafts coming through?
Well, I'll keep her warm tonight!

The Inuit make fire with their bow and drill
but I've got a different drill to set the little lady aflame.

He was so keen to be with the woman he forgot to seal one small chink.

Just a minute

The fox-wife hadn't realised the wife-swap was to happen immediately.
She'd gone to sleep in the normal way and then the wolverine woke her.

He sniffed her, snuggled himself in close, as if they were husband and
    wife,
the kind who'd shared a hunting life together for many a year.

Still asleep, almost immediately she knew something was wrong,
but it must be a nightmare and all she had to do was shout out "No!"

She'd wake and Kiviuq would protect her.
"No!" she said,

and then she was awake and saw it was the wolverine mauling her.
She shuddered, drew back in shock. "Kiviuq! Help!" But he doesn't come.

And then she realised what had happened:
the trade was tonight. It was legitimate, it was tradition.

Playing for time she said to the animal, "Please, I'll sleep with you,
but first I need to answer nature's call. Look away, sir."

She went over to that part of the iglu and crouched down.

Waterfall

Disobeying Kiviuq, the wolverine watched at a distance,
enjoying the sound and look of the little yellow waterfall
as it tumbled gently from between the fox-wife's legs.

He came over to her just as she was finishing
and she flinched, shuddered again.

"Wait!" he said, sniffing the air, catching the scent of the pee.
"You're a dirty fox!"

A simple matter

"You're a dirty fox!" he said
and how many times have my kind been called that.

He spat his words at me and I was almost ashamed of what I am
but every curse needs the fear of the cursed.
Why should any creature be compelled to deny their nature?
Why should any creature be denied the possibility of a better future?

It was a simple matter.
I walked over to my bundle, unwrapped my fox-skin and clothed myself in it.
Since, as easily as finding blood on snow,
I could detect the stream of fresh air pouring through the gash in the wall,
I rushed at the blocks weakened by the gap.
I burst through and made my escape.

Outside

Kiviuq hadn't gone into the wolverine's home.
It reeked and he wasn't sure if the stench
was the squalor of the wolverine and his wife
or the stink of his own betrayal.

Practically a family

When the wolverine came shuffling out he was angry with Kiviuq.
"After all the help I gave you, you trick me with a fox!"

"We are practically family," he went on,
"and you try to dupe me with a cunning little bitch!"

Kiviuq guessed the wolverine had broken every pledge
but there was no time for justice. He set off after the fox-wife.

The wolverine returned to his own iglu
and who knows what he did next in there.

Slits

The hunter fastens the goggles tight to the face.

There's a single slit to cut back on reflection – long
to see everything.

Tracking

Kiviuq moved quickly tracking the fox-wife.
Where she had urinated he licked it up.
Where she had defecated he ate it up.

The low house

Kiviuq came to a low house and for a second
he thought he'd arrived back home –
wasn't this the grave of the young woman
he had murdered with fire?

Beauty contest

A lemming in the form of a woman is there at the entrance,
petite, small ears. "My, you're a big fella," she says,
"Would you care to share my bunk?"

"That's kind of you," Kiviuq replies, "but I've heard you bruise easily."

A weasel in the form of a woman takes her place,
"Welcome," she says, "would you like to hold me close, tonight?"

"No offence," Kiviuq replies, "but you're just too skinny for my tastes."
A siksik (that's a ground squirrel) appears and Kiviuq isn't sure if it's a
    woman
or a man. "I'm yours, if you want me," they say.

"You're lovely," Kiviuq says, "but you're on the roundy side for me."

An arctic hare replaces the siksik – the short white fur on top of their
    head
reminds Kiviuq of his wife's thicker snowy tresses.

"Sorry," Kiviuq tells her, "it's your eyes, they're just too distant from each
    other."
A wolverine comes out of the shadow of the door
and no it's not Kiviuq's old 'friend' though he has to look at her twice.

"I'm just not in the mood, lady," Kiviuq tells her and she goes back in.

Now there's a raven-woman and Kiviuq likes her shiny black coat
but the smell on her breath is dirty.

"Good to meet you, but I'm afraid I am not fond of your perfume."

Next in the beauty contest is a tall fulmar-woman and Kiviuq likes her
   cute beak.
"Come with me and we can fly away to our own private island," she tells
   him,

but she falls off the chair she's been standing on and Kiviuq just shakes
   his head.

Finally, the handsome grey form of a wolf-woman appears at the door.
"You look ravenous," she says, making eye contact, "for company,
and I'm in heat."

Tempted

Kiviuq is shocked. The wolf is far too forward for his liking...

but maybe she has the brusque purity of honesty – his heart is beating
    faster,
their eye-contact is flirtatious, she touches his shoulder.
She is strong, like his first wife (and she was a wolf, too).
He, or a part of him, is persuaded by her.
Yes, they have a common future.
Equals in nature should make alliances together.

He's thinking much clearer, he's moved in closer,
he's taking in her scent. Her stature, her charisma
(her aroma's an event), such a sublime creature! This match was meant!
After all he's endured to be here why shouldn't he enjoy at least a night here,
savour every inch of her, every feature. It would be rude
to refuse, an affront to withhold consent, it would be 'lose lose'.
It's just common sense to sleep with the wolf.

Decision

"No," he says, finally.

"It's the snout," he says, improvising,
tapping his own nose to indicate the wolf's
but remembering every detail of the face
of the fox-wife, how refined she was
in form and manner, how much he misses her.

"I'm sorry," he says, "It's nothing personal."
But the she-wolf has already gone.

Brief instruction

The lemming-woman Kiviuq had seen at the doorway reappeared.
"Well done," she said, "Now turn around, close your eyes
and walk backwards into our home."

The party

I heard it from Tapeesa who heard it from Kallik
who heard it from Kareama who was there with Uki
and they say Pana was there as well, with Panuk and even Silla.
Not often you see Silla under the earth.

Kiviuq arrived backwards and when he turned around
he saw all the animals bringing portions of meat to the party.
"No stealing!" everyone was shouting as Wolf and Wolverine walked in
with a shoulder of caribou on each of their shoulders.

It was obvious it was booty from a meat cache
but they weren't having it, "I got this fair and square," Wolf said
and Wolverine even stole bits off of Wolf's sentence,
growling to the crowd, "Square and fair!".
In the end, no-one was in the mood to challenge them too hard
and you could see it was fine caribou.

Four bears came in briefly, a man-bear with only one leg
and a bear-woman rubbing a huge scar on her stomach.
They and their two cubs each brought an arctic char.
Pana was talking with them about starting a new life.

Raven came in with a turd in her beak, calling out in a gabble,
"This is delicious and there's plenty more where this came from!"
The crowd were disgusted and shouted, "Get that out of here!"

As Raven was leaving she bumped into Hare and the Siksiks
who had all brought nibbles.
They turned away from Raven
and soon settled down for the start of the song contest.

"Just look at Wolverine!" Wolf began, "A pint-sized grizzly
whose idea of hunting is snatching scraps from a human's meat cache."
"Just Listen to the Great Hunter!" Wolverine replied, "An overgrown fox
who once tripped himself up running after Hare – she escaped in one
    bound!"

Hare nodded nervously, looking at Wolf – "That's not untrue," she sang
    cautiously,
"but I want you to know I'm not prejudiced against hunters who are
    lame."

At that point Gull walked in with Raven, who had nothing in her beak
    now,
and immediately Raven started on her companion,
"Just look at that mucky-white jacket of yours," she sang,
"and they say I'm the dirty one!"

Gull wasn't having that, "Everyone knows you're just a seagull covered in
    soot!
Anyway, who cares what my clothes are like,
when the ice breaks up on the river
it's my beak that spears the salmon in the water below.
Raven, you're just a hunter of left-overs, of washed-up scum,
of those brown-slop creatures who slip out comatose
from the pucker of a straining arse!"

The crowd loved Seagull's song and were amazed that Raven
    immediately had a response,
"It's all very well, Chancer, when warm weather gives you a helping claw
and the salmon leap into your beak, but you go hungry when the river
    freezes over!"
Several in the crowd murmured agreement, "She's got you there, Seagull,
you're a skeleton in winter!"

"You should learn from the likes of me," Raven went on as Seagull struggled
    to reply,
"There'd be a bright future for you and everyone in this cavern
if only you'd eat shite!"

Though all there were included in Raven's accusation,
everyone roared with laughter. You had to concede she had won the
    competition!
Seagull agreed and smiled at his half-sister.
It was time to eat what had been brought to the get-together –
and Raven may have won the contest but her delicacies were still not allowed
    in the hall!
For a full merry hour all the rivals feasted as friends.

Finally, Kiviuq, whose diet had not been the best lately,
farted – and that was the end of the party.

In the small cave

When the air had cleared Kiviuq sought out his wife
and found her in a small cave low down in the underworld.
She had been crying so hard and so long
that the tears and the drops from her nose had combined
and solidified, forming a stalactite which fixed her to the cave floor.

Kiviuq approached and she flinched. She tried to move away from him,
but the stalactite was jail bar and pinion.

He thought for a moment and then composed
a large gob of spit in his mouth.
He was beginning an incantation of liquid silver.

First he sloshed the spit in his mouth with a slapping rhythm
left and right, front and back,

then he gargled with it,
making a sound that would almost rival
any woman expert in throat-singing, in the art of "Katadjak".

Finally he spat this glinting song of sacred water
right at his wife.

The stalactite shattered.

Exit

Kiviuq's wife embraced him
but this reunion, though tender, was as sombre as many a last parting.

Quietly they climbed up towards ordinary Earth.
The fox-wife went first along the narrow passageways
and as they approached the entrance a creature in the shadows,
having let the fox-wife pass unharmed, jumped on to Kiviuq's back.

It scratched him to the bone before he threw it to the floor.
He turned and was about to kick it, to stomp it to death
(as they say one mother once killed her simple son
knowing there would be too little food for both of them that winter).
Then he saw it was a being who had suffered burns the full length of its body.
It was more ash than flesh.

He stopped his boot from smashing its skull
and just before he turned to exit the grave-like home
his eyes met the eyes of the charcoal creature.
He thought he recognised the woman he had murdered with fire.

The entrance is closing.
"Hurry! The entrance is closing," he heard the fox-wife calling.
There was no time to articulate sorrow
or, if his instincts were right and he had once been married to the shadow,
to offer any botch of an explanation.
He ran on towards the surface and had to turn sideways as the opening
    contracted.
Only by breathing in sharply did he make it safely to his wife above
and to the wide bright light of the day.

10

THE GOOSE

If you live for thousands of years

If you live for thousands of years
is love for ordinary mortals foolish?
Is it love? Do you protect yourself
by trying not to love?

Can tenderness only find comprehension
between creatures promised death soon enough?
Can love only exist between ordinary creatures
who cherish the fragile lives they share?

At the lake

at first it's sound he hears:
two women laughing,
a splish
   and now
        a splash,

talking serious
then enjoying nonsense

now letting silence
hear itself think.

Soon, crouching,
unseen, he sees them:
     standing,
      confidential,
         then swimming together

                out to the centre

Clothes on the shore

Two sets of clothes on a rock,
high enough up to avoid any wake.

They are suits of feathers from two water-birds:
a swan and a goose. They even have little stockings.

The swan

Kiviuq gathers the swan's bundle of clothes
and holds them up as if he has made her image from snow.

The swan-woman swims calmly toward him
and is soon out of the water, dark eyes, lips of yellow.

"Why are you playing these games," she says, "a grown man?
Which of your puny arms would you like me to break first?"

Kiviuq hands her the suit of feathers.
He tries to tease her by holding back her stockings

but one look from the swan and he simply hands them over.

The goose

Kiviuq gathers the goose's bundle of clothes
and holds them up as if he has made her image from rock.

The goose-woman swims frantically toward him
and is soon out of the water, dark eyes, lips of black.

"Please, give me back my suit of feathers," she says,
    distraught.
 "I am naked! Why are you, a grown man, so cruel!"

Kiviuq hands her the suit of feathers, stockings and all.

Kiviuq's call

Several years later and can you hear Kiviuq's call –
"Aasiggai, aasiggai, aasi, aasi, aasiggai.
Here I am! I'm home!" –

and two human-like children
run out to see their father.

Just outside the door is the goose-woman.
Just inside is the hunter's mother.

It's not a criticism

Remember when that goose of a woman
laid four eggs and straightaway you broke two open,
slurping their goodness into your belly.
That was the last time Nirliq did you any favours.

Just between me and you

While Nirliq is down by the shore,
let me tell you something, son,
she still eats nothing but grass and grit!
And she's taught the children
to eat nothing else.

"Stones or grain, stones or grain!"
You could bring all the seals in the sea home to us
and still she'd make sure your family fed on sand.

Holes between the fingers

Look, mother, the holes between our fingers have grown larger.
Look, mother, the holes between our fingers have grown deeper.

Here are eight feathers, daughter.
Here are eight feathers, son.
Practice behind the iglu, out of sight of anyone.

Flight

Kiviuq is in his kayak out on the open sea.
The snow bunting keeps him safe.

Kiviuq is at an ice-hole out on the pack ice.
The polar bear keeps him safe.

Why, Kiviuq is thinking, does he have to live with his dead
    mother?
Why, Kiviuq is thinking, can't he finally be allowed peace?

He doesn't notice and then he notices three geese in the
    distance, flying south.

Waterfowl

"Where's the family?" Kiviuq asks
and his mother flinches.

"If you mean the waterfowl you tamed
didn't you see all three of them flying off?"

"You can't go against nature, son."

Silaup putunga
(The hole in the universe)

Let me tell you about
the hole in the universe –
when you find the right tune
the lives of the world will bend to your will.

You can slip past time.
Places travel and you stay still.

I travel by song

I'm travelling to the place where there's no winter,
walking will take too long.
I'm travelling alone to find where I belong.
I'm following the birds. I travel by song.

The ocean's an oil lamp.
I dance on chunks of blubber to get along.
I'm following the birds. I travel by song.

The ocean's a soup pot.
I dance on chunks of meat to get along.
I'm following the birds. I travel by song.

I see mountains clashing.
I head straight through and on.
I'm following the birds. I travel by song.

I see grizzlies fighting –
I slip between them as they play on.
I'm following the birds. I travel by song.

A woman's torso gets on top of me,
we make love and I move on.
I'm following the birds. I travel by song.

A man's torso gets on top of me,
we make love and I move on.
I'm following the birds. I travel by song.

I'm travelling to the place where there's no winter,
walking will take too long.
I'm travelling alone to find where I belong.
I'm following the birds. I travel by song.

The giant

When Kiviuq came out of the hole in the universe
he was close to another shore. He had stopped singing.

In the middle distance there was a huge naked man
roughly chipping away at an uprooted tree with an axe.

He would take each wood chip and rub it against his penis.
He'd throw each fleck of wood into the sea and each became a salmon.

The giant had his back to Kiviuq
and as he got closer he could see he was hollow:

his mouth went in a tunnel straight to the hole in his backside.

He might be sensitive about that, Kiviuq thought to himself,
and made sure he approached him from side on.

"Hullo, stranger," said the giant, tensing his hands round the tree,
"you didn't come up from behind, did you?"

"No, Sir," said Kiviuq, "I've come from this direction."

Can you help me?

When Kiviuq explained he needed to cross the vast stretch of ocean
to be with his wife and children, the giant said "I will help you."
He beckoned to a fish skeleton in the ocean and it came to the shore.
"Hold on to the fin on this creature's back night and day and you will be safe.
When you are finally near shallow water it will tremble with excitement
and you must let go and walk through the water to the land.
Put your ear to the ground and you will hear your family."

Kiviuq clambered on to the skeleton and it changed into a huge salmon.
He thanked the giant and travelled night and day with his hands on the fin.
When the fish shuddered with energy Kiviuq thanked the fish and stepped off
into shallow water. The fish was a fin and then a moving shadow and then
gone.

Reunion

As he walked through the water to shore
Kiviuq saw his old kayak floating towards him
guided by the snow bunting.

Landfall

He made landfall and the air was full of bird calls.
There were no birds to be seen.
He remembered what the giant had told him
and put his ear to the ground.
He could hear his children's voices, distinct.

He began walking in their direction
and made his call – "Aasiggai, aasiggai, aasi, aasi, aasiggai.
Here I am!"

In no time at all he saw his children in human form almost flying to him.

Remarried

Kiviuq had been gone a few minutes in song time
but years in a life.

The goose-wife had remarried.
She'd chosen another goose, to make life simpler.
When one of her children brought the news
she thought the boy was ill.
Then she heard Kiviuq's call – "I am here"
and she knew it was true.

Her husband was afraid but said, "Don't worry,
Kiviuq is not the kind of man to harm anyone."
All the same he fled far from their home
and away from the settlement of birds.
He had to rush back, explaining to everyone,
"I forgot my tool box, I forgot my tool box!"

He'd left his guts at home.
Tucking them back into his body he took a run at the sky,
took flight, and was never seen again.

Beads and mitts

He gives me beads and mitts
and I thank him and set them gently aside.

How did he travel so far,
beyond the 'second step'?

He gives me beads and mitts
and I thank him and set them gently aside.

"I am here," he says,
a child, a man, Kiviuq,

and I hold him for a time.

Have you seen Kiviuq?

Have you seen Kiviuq?

I heard he moved to the far south.
I heard he followed the birds when they flew to the summer lands.
I heard he settled at the shore where the seas don't freeze.

Greenland and Iceland would be stepping stones to Kivuq!
Maybe he is living beyond the second step, in Scotland?

I heard he is slowly becoming stone. Lichen has settled on his face
and these days he doesn't like to be among people.

Have you seen Kiviuq? Is this just the start of his story?

AFTERWORD
by Nancy Campbell

While this book was in preparation, a solo exhibition by the renowned Iqaluit-based artist and jeweller Mathew Nuqingaq opened in Toronto. Many of the works in *Masquerade* riffed on the snow goggles traditionally worn by Inuit and Yupik hunters: a band strapped across the eyes, which lessens the amount of light reaching the retina, reducing the risk of snow blindness. The dazzling effect of the glare of sun on Arctic ice is a metaphor which may be understood differently by those schooled in the European literary tradition, aware of blind Homer giving voice to Odysseus' epic voyages, and the trope of visual impairment as sign of a capacity for otherworldly visions. Nuqingaq's artefacts are elegantly re-envisioned for the contemporary urban hunter: spectacles and lorgnettes to be looked *at* or admired as much as looked through. The modest wood or bone plaque with its iconic horizontal slit is replaced by polished, finely etched steel, forged in familiar styles: hippy circles, pointed cat eyes or wraparounds. They speak not so much to ocular protection, as the significance of the eyes when it comes to disguising the face. In another epic, the tale of Kiviuq in these pages, a boy is dressed by his grandmother in the skin of the first seal he catches. The "delicate" shape of the seal's eyes fits perfectly over the boy's own. Those who deal with skins well know this quality of the eye-holes – when skin is flensed from the animal, and flattened into a one-dimensional field, the spaces where the eyes once were is the only survival of a face that in life was "pierced with greedy holes."

Today many eyes in the urban strongholds of the West are trained greedily on the Arctic, a region of increasing geopolitical importance. Those who hunt its riches may come in helicopters, with drills and rigs, instead of the boats and harpoons described in these pages. Meanwhile, environmental changes are well documented: in Russia's melting permafrost long-frozen viruses such as anthrax are reviving; in Greenland snowmelt is exposing biological, chemical and radioactive waste from the former US Cold War airbase, Camp Century; everywhere there is accelerated sea ice melt and glacier retreat. As human-induced climate crisis imperils the polar environment, those living elsewhere (including many who have benefitted from the lifestyles that contribute to the catastrophe) cannot afford to be complacent. These issues do not concern the Arctic alone: sea level rise already affects cities and small island nations around the globe. But who is the owner of the sea?

A number of nations, including Britain, sent expeditions north in the nineteenth century hoping to take control of sea routes through the Arctic ice. While many failed to achieve their objectives, few explorers missed the opportunity to publish sensational memoirs of their journeys, with illustrations depicting tall-masted vessels among sublime icescapes. These reports became the lens through which people living at more southerly latitudes imagined the Arctic. Now documentaries and newspaper reports recycle a seductive image of pristine ice and wilderness under threat, for immediate social media likes, but little action. Local hunters are enlisted to provide plangent soundbites, detailing changes to traditional lifestyles, but all too rarely do media outlets allow them to tell the full story. The Arctic has always been a region claimed, named and changed by those passing through it; today that number includes artists, scientists, and those employed seasonally in the tourism or mining industries.

The character and extent of historic Inuit presence in the Arctic is evident in the journeys described in these poems. In his first voyage, Kiviuq paddles the ocean for three days before he encounters land. Like the British naval officers and other *qallunaat*, he is an explorer, who joins with his sled's traces and kayak's wake the most remote (to him) and unknown corners of the world, always going "further further further". In a wry reversal of those other explorers' journeys, Price wonders whether Kiviuq may have come closer than we might think: "Greenland and Iceland would be stepping stones to Kiviuq! / Maybe he is living beyond the second step, in Scotland?" Sometimes Kiviuq travelled to escape something or someone, sometimes to find something or someone. Sometimes it was just time to move on.

"I heard he followed the birds when they flew to the summer lands. / I heard he settled at the shore where the seas don't freeze." In communities across the Inuit world, from Greenland to Alaska, people migrate to places where animals can be found at specific seasons. Survival is dependent on avoiding starvation, which in turn means being in the right place at the right time. Knowledge of location and migration routes is passed on from generation to generation. The writer Barry Lopez describes these routes as "corridors of breath", a fitting expression for the regular and vital nature of the journeys made along them. The telling of tales has synchronicities with the sharing of trails, both activities now moving from speech onto paper and screen. *Kiviuq's Journey*, which Price uses as source material, is an online resource. Another recent research project, the pan-Inuit Trails Atlas, presents those journeys as a means of underscoring Inuit sovereignty in the Canadian Arctic. Once the ice had melted or there was a fresh snowfall or water closed behind the kayak, the trail was gone – but today's researcher can view them again in the intricate layers of the online atlas. Cartographic sources are just one way to establish evidence of Inuit journeys; others include archaeology and oral history, such as the travels and transgressions of Sedna and Kiviuq and the Old Woman who changed herself into a man. Richard Price's versions of these narrative tales make the cultural history of this region available to new audiences. Legends offer complex layers just like the digital maps do, as the narrator points out from time to time. At these moments Price boldly opts for multiplicity, so that valency lies with the reader as much as the teller. Reading these poems – noting subtle shifts in time and place and personhood – feels very different to following a surfaced highway.

In deliberate contrast to earlier expeditions seeking trade routes, the Greenlandic-Danish polar explorer Knud Rasmussen organised a "Literary Expedition" to the Arctic in the early twentieth century. While the First World War devastated central Europe, his small team travelled north by sled up the Greenlandic coast and across the icy expanses of Nunavut, gathering traditional knowledge from the people he encountered. He was told a version of the Sedna story, which is included in the five volumes of material he published later. He describes gatherings in a song tent – the sweat of close-packed, anticipatory bodies; his vision dimmed in air thick with smoke from blubber lamps. "From the very first, the tunes are riveting and carry us away," he wrote. "I can understand more clearly than ever, how difficult it is to take the songs of the Eskimos [sic] out of their own context. For the words of the songs are only part of the whole intended effect." It was not only due to the smoky dimness of the venue that Rasmussen found it difficult to record the songs in his notebook. He later acknowledged that his own "neat written language and... sober orthography... couldn't bestow sufficient form or force" on the singers' words. Yet Rasmussen had briefly worked as an opera singer in Copenhagen; he was no stranger to words moving between page and performance. Subsequent translators of Rasmussen (such as Tom Lowenstein, whose text I quote here) echo his concerns. How to evoke the powerful musicality and temporality of the original? The tale is passed on, and in the telling inevitably altered. The singer or storyteller is reminiscent of Sedna's dog-husband, who must swim faithfully between the shores on which different generations live, carrying provisions from father to daughter in his jaws – and hoping not to drop the gifts or indeed drown in the strong currents.

The poems in *The Owner of the Sea* are not translations but versions of existing translations, and Richard Price is careful to clarify their status as such. He employs narrative interjections to pull the original closer, at the same time as emphasizing its separateness from the reader's experience: "*tuutaliit* – you'll have a word for it in your language". Rasmussen observed that in Inuit culture "Words (like snow, or bones, or reindeer skin) are part of the material environment, and they have the sort of concrete property which can be woven, wrapped up, carved and put together, for either functional or aesthetic purposes.' It is good to find some vestiges of them here. Yet there is more to poetry than its vocabulary. "True translation," wrote John Berger, "is not a binary affair between two languages but a triangular affair. The third point of the triangle being what lay behind the words of the original text before it was written. True translation demands a return to the pre-verbal.' Price honours the pre-verbal essence, and in his hands it shapeshifts, takes on modern guise. Unlike some previously published North American versions of Rasmussen's texts which were bowdlerised or self-consciously naïve or archaic, these texts wear their new garb with pride. For example, Price introduces the language of relationship counselling, emphasizes the fluidity of gender and leaves Kiviuq's sexuality open-ended. It is also topical that these narratives celebrate the potential of human relations with the natural world, or the more-than-human: women take dogs and fulmars as lovers, men partner with foxes and geese; bears shed their skins to become human; and even a bit of sweet-smelling driftwood has enough agency to keep two women satisfied.

The narrator of Kiviuq's tale, like the protagonist himself, is a trickster. His sardonic voice is demarked from the main narrative by parentheses: "[don't ask / what Kiviuq deserves or if he's sorry – we're not in that kind of world / are we?]" Thus the reader is jolted out of the world of the story from time to time, just as Kiviuq himself seems unable to settle down in any singular narrative. These are the conventions of Inuit song, even if the specifics are the poet's invention: repetition; multiple points of view; dizzying shifts in time. Literary techniques like these speak to a culture more engaged in the potential of multiplicity than singular truths; they evoke the haphazard patterns of memory, rather than the dogma of linear time. The timeline of these poems shifts forwards and backwards like a rogue escalator, tumbling and staggering those characters who ride it, not to mention the reader. In the midst of his adventures Kiviuq tantalisingly "remembers meeting another woman / a long time before all this began." Yet, at the very beginning of the sequence, Price asks: "Is his story coming to an end?"

Locations are unpredictable too. Sedna and Kiviuq are outsiders, who pause their travels to become members of a community for only a short while. Indeed there are so many outsiders in these texts that the idea of a centre existing at all is exploded. Kiviuq lives for a while in what the narrator describes with an ironic shrug of apostrophes as "marginal territories", the margins of the margins he has already travelled through, but inevitably ever his own centre ("places travel and you stay still"). He is a serial neighbour. Hospitality is vital in this region, but often comes vexed with complications, as Kiviuq finds when Wolverine helps him to build a snow house. The host may pose a threat, but so too can a guest. While Sedna's and Kiviuq's experiences are defined by their travels through place, *The Old Woman who changed herself into a Man* explores the journeys made by those who remain behind. The women's story begins with the departure of the men in the community, and it ends (in every sense) with the arrival of a single, male stranger. The visitor's prurient presence causes a regressive transformation in the Old Woman, yet the reader relies on his witness: "he is the reason you and everyone else knows our story." In this sleight of hand, which reveals the unwelcome guest as a proxy for the narrator, Price adroitly addresses the question of voyeurism and the issue of theft. What happens when someone's story is "seen" by outsiders?

Dressing and undressing convey critical moments in these tales; for example, clothes are left carefully folded at the lake shore when characters bathe, or get up to other activities in the water. A woman kills her daughter in order to take her place in Kiviuq's affections, and wears the daughter's skin as a disguise, but the wrinkles where it gathers around her hips give her away. Just as words have a concrete property (as Rasmussen observes above), so skins, stones and other artefacts convey a message. Stones arranged in human shape become a teller of trails, "a man / made of stones, the way-marker they call an inukshuk". The inukshuk were both part of the landscape and also communicated its character, before maps and "neat written language". It is noted that Kiviuq and an inukshuk he passes on his journey have nothing to say to each other – but that in itself constitutes a relationship. In fact, they are very closely related: Kiviuq will subsequently emulate the attributes of an inukshuk, when he hides behind one to observe his future fox-wife. Price ventures further in his coda to Kiviuq's tale, imagining that the legendary traveller may become one of the settled, silent way-markers: "I hear he is slowly becoming stone. Lichen has settled on his face…" The status of the tales has changed too, settled down, grown silent; no longer songs to be heard, more often books to be held in the hands and read. On the page sight overcomes sound, as in that moment of encounter, when Kiviuq and the fox-wife assess each other for the first time: "Silence. / Eyes / meeting eyes." There are eyes that warn and curse as well as eyes that seduce: the eyes of the dead brothers, bobbing in the Bee Woman's cooking pot; the look the Bee Woman gives Kiviuq, which causes him to faint ("Is she a spirit? They say you can tell by looking at the eyes"). Meanwhile Kiviuq keeps an eye out for the snow bunting (his familiar) who knows the way ahead for a kayak, even across the ice or through a storm. *Follow the birds, travel by song:* the reader's eyes sweep across the tracks of letters on the page.

And yet *The Owner of the Sea* arises from a tradition intensely engaged with the question of how to best to tell a narrative, and what the listener might do with the words they are given. Price's poems acknowledge this heritage by repeatedly referring to the power of words, the act of speech. Sedna forges her own narrative from the outset by refusing the suitors who are offered to her: "She keeps saying No." Speech defies, and it also holds the power of persuasion. Sedna says: "send me a hunter, a powerful singer". Yet the courtship song of the Fulmar she falls for is spellbinding in another sense; a masquerade, even: "the right song disguises any creature. When he sang he was a man to me, more than any local boy". Song seduces, and it also holds the potential of salvation. In the end, it is Kiviuq's singing that will shatter an icy stalactite and free his fox-wife from the underworld. Whether song also has the power to restore ice in the world above is a question to which no one can know the answer.

Notes

1. *Mathew Nuqingaq: Masquerade*, 13 June – 13 July 2019, Feheley Fine Arts, 65 George Street, Ontario, M5A4L8, Canada.

2. Jean Paul Sartre, 'Faces', *Essays in Phenomenology*, quoted in 'An interview with Lena Herzog', *Believer Magazine* 81, 2001.

3. Barry Lopez, *Arctic Dreams*, Chapter five, 'Migration: The Corridors of Breath', Scribner: New York, 1986.

4. "The Atlas is one of the outcomes of the project 'The Northwest Passage and the construction of Inuit pan-Arctic identities' (funded by SSHRC—the Social Sciences and Humanities Research Council), and co-directed by Claudio Aporta (Marine Affairs Program, Dalhousie University), Michael Bravo (Geography, University of Cambridge), and Fraser Taylor (Geomatics and Cartographic Research Centre, Carleton University). This project looks at Inuit occupancy of the Northwest Passage, through a study and documentation of Inuit traditional trails and place names, which have interconnected Inuit groups across the Arctic since time immemorial." http://www.paninuittrails.org

5. Rasmussen, trans. Tom Lowenstein, *Eskimo Poems*, Allison & Busby: London, 1973, p. 109.

6. Lowenstein, *Eskimo Poems*, p. xxii.

7. John Berger, 'Self Portrait', *Confabulations*, p.4. Penguin: London, 2016.